Echoing Reflection

Michael Rosé

Introduction
The concept of the Echoing Reflection is the idea of constant self examination, and finding the same things time and time again. These poems are what I have found within my personal reflections and examining the people and the world around me.

Acknowledgements
Firstly to both Andy Jackson (photographer) and Urania Brown (model) for helping with the cover.
Mr Guy (English teacher) who introduced me to poetry. Chris Harding for all his help. Finally to various members of my family and friends for their part in the making of this book.

Contact
www.myspace.com/mrose_poetry
mrose_poetry@hotmail.co.uk

ISBN: 978-0-9559839-0-0

Copyright © Michael Rosé 2007-2008

Biography

Michael started off his writing from the age of 16 as a songwriter, but after a short while realised that he enjoyed crafting the lyrics to songs more than the music and began work as a poet. He pursued these early days of writing under the name "Forever Dying", being a name to describe the feelings and emotions he expressed in his early poems. Initially trying to find a crowd for his poetry, finding he was creating websites in an effort to show it to his friends.

Developing his style and love for the written word, he started to read about poetry and the poems of other writers collecting ideas on how to shape his work. During this time he was still playing music with Artisian.

After many years of putting together a catalogue of work, by September 2007 he compiled a self published collection of 35 poems entitled "Redemption Song", but with no great success.

Now with his second collection, "Echoing Reflection", incorporating poems that were written in the same period of time as "Redemption song", as well as others that have been written in the period since.

Introduction
The concept of the Echoing Reflection is the idea of constant self examination, and finding the same things time and time again. These poems are what I have found within my personal reflections and examining the people and the world around me.

Acknowledgements
Firstly to both Andy Jackson (photographer) and Urania Brown (model) for helping with the cover.
Mr Guy (English teacher) who introduced me to poetry. Chris Harding for all his help. Finally to various members of my family and friends for their part in the making of this book.

Contact
www.myspace.com/mrose_poetry
mrose_poetry@hotmail.co.uk

ISBN: 978-0-9559839-0-0

Copyright © Michael Rosé 2007-2008

Biography

Michael started off his writing from the age of 16 as a songwriter, but after a short while realised that he enjoyed crafting the lyrics to songs more than the music and began work as a poet. He pursued these early days of writing under the name "Forever Dying", being a name to describe the feelings and emotions he expressed in his early poems. Initially trying to find a crowd for his poetry, finding he was creating websites in an effort to show it to his friends.

Developing his style and love for the written word, he started to read about poetry and the poems of other writers collecting ideas on how to shape his work. During this time he was still playing music with Artisian.

After many years of putting together a catalogue of work, by September 2007 he compiled a self published collection of 35 poems entitled "Redemption Song", but with no great success.

Now with his second collection, "Echoing Reflection", incorporating poems that were written in the same period of time as "Redemption song", as well as others that have been written in the period since.

Contents

Echoing Reflection	6
Phantom Audience	7
Funeral Bride	8
The Abyss	8
Leads Me Back (To)	9
Fallen Petal	10
Camden Testimony	11
Culture Of The Vulture	13
All The Rage	14
By Candlelight	15
Stolen Moments And The Assassin	16
Flight Of The Raven	17
I Am The Raven	18
Letting Go	19
Wishing Life Away	20
House Of Cards	21
The Hanging Disappointment	22
The Face Of Redemption	23
Screaming Through A Stitched Mouth	24
Dreaming Blind	25
Anhedonic	26
Elmers End	27
Stabbed To Death (In The Sun)	28
Minerva's Reverie	29
Good Morning My Someone	30
Sea Of Fire	31
Misery	32
The Angel Of Darkness	33
Of Forever Dying	34
Final Goodbye (For Now)	35
Until The End	36

Echoing Reflection

The echoing reflection of the face of redemption, with crimson tears and hollow fears ripples through history of emotions left unsaid

A revolving thought of false lives are taught, creating recreations in trials and trepidations in the words that are bled

Forever dying and always crying, diminished by hatred until we are sedated by subliminal rage dragging us through hesitation

Ever is the lasting, dangerous in our catharting as we end our lives in our demise through our freefalling obsession.

Phantom Audience

What started off as heaven,
Fell into the hell I was running from
I can still smell my self pity
I can still see my anxiety
I can still feel my rage
I can still hear my misery

Am I holding on to what I left behind?
Am I looking for something that's not there for me to find?
The taste on my lips from the blood that's been spilled, cries
out in agony of how much of a fool I am
My heightened senses, I thought would pull me out of who I am
and never wanted to be
Living amongst a world that never wanted me

I'm stillborn but still walking into the unseen, forever Eden
never again
As the ink dries out from my pen
Infamy is too good for me
But blasphemy would be better
The hanging tree is calling me
But who would read my letter?

My phantom audience have left me for dead
For everything I ever wrote and everything they never read
These words gather with dust
But no one seems to be fussed, about it

Funeral Bride

Everybody knows, everybody dies
But no one knows more than the funeral bride
Standing there lifeless with her hands by her side
Wondering "when will it be my time?"

The Abyss

I'm standing on the edge, starring into the abyss. The abyss is staring back daring me to fall.

Leads Me Back (To)

Life, neatly in ruins
Possessed, by perusing
Death, I can't control
Everything, in its whole
Nothing, ever survives
Obsession, which is my drive
Avoiding, in which I lack
Confidence, which leads me back

Fallen Petal

The fallen petal
Withers and fades
Out from the sunshine
And into the shade

Out from public gaze
Or from interaction
Shame over compensating
For its black haze

Fading into the soil
To breathe life into the new
To spawn more flowers
That will only be seen by a few

So that the fallen
Can have its peace
And the newly blossomed
Can go on in place

Camden Testimony

Upon a midnight dreary
I'm not thinking very clearly
Whether I should stay or go
The last train draws near
The night bus I fear
Because if I died who would know?

The drink has started flowing
And I don't know where I'm going
Maybe one more will settle my head
But before I realised
A shot has materialised
One more, the its time for bed

Great, now I feel sick
That hasn't done the trick
I can't head home feeling like this
The songs are blaring
What is she wearing?
Maybe I should sneak in a kiss

Well that didn't work
I feel like a berk
But the night's not over yet
Maybe one more beer
Then my thoughts will be clear
Because that girl's boyfriend looks upset

It's starting to get late
And I'm in a shocking state
I wonder where we're off next
Whose place is free?
Who could we go see?

Because standing up right now is too complex

There's nowhere we can stay
It's not long till the train
Now its time to head back
I'll get some beers for the way there
And tomorrow I'll take care
Because my liver can't handle another attack

As I stagger down the street
I can't see my feet
As I climb the stairs to the platform
I try to understand
Why I can't stand
I hope the train isn't too long

I've woken up again
At London Bridge station
And managed to stay out all night
Where the hell have I been?
Whose faces have I seen?
I really should have left at midnight

Culture Of The Vulture

What has happened to the world we live in?
When did living a life you enjoy become a sin?
There once was a time when being oversized was a sign of wealth
Now everyone wants to risk their mind, their body and health
To fit into a stick thin media frenzied nation
When the rest of the time we're trying to stop Africa from starvation
Does this irony make any sense when all is said and done?
We are not born a skeleton, why must we portray one?
Being Rubenesque is still something to admire and revere
Not a sign of neglect or hatred of self and fear
If love truly exists sure it's more than just aesthetics
If that's all it is, then it's nothing short of pathetic
Is this something so superficial that we all strive for?
Well if it is, no one should have any part of it anymore
Because what happens to those who can't meet the expectations?
I guess they must fade away from this starving nation
Certainly we can't accept this as some sort of culture
Because the only ones who win are the ones portraying vultures

All The Rage

All the rage I feel and fear
Rises up to my throat
Making it evidently clear
That my thoughts won't make it over the moat

My thoughts have gone from king to jester
From being heard to being a joke
They just seem to pester
I made it to the moat but they've been left to soak

Drowning in my recurring self pity
For this you always know
I may have changed city
But I wait for my inhibitions to let go

Waiting for the jester to become king
The moments will come, you always knew
The redemption song we will sing
As I suffer at the hands of all of you

By Candlelight

By candlelight
I live through the night
Open, naked and exposed

Watching the shadows of light flicker
Being guardian of the man made wicker
And those who are prevalent to be foes

A beautiful mourning to those who've died
In comparison to those who've tried
To die, from grace

As angels they'll fall
Making angels of us all
As the pieces of the puzzle fall into place

The wind of death blows the light away
And I'm left with nothing left to say
But I' m left in the shadow s to cry

And in this shadow despair
Screaming we don't care
Are left the candlelight to die

Stolen Moments And The Assassin

I've always wondered what could've been
All the times we could've had and all the things we could've done
All the great places and people we've seen
Any moments like these to happen again, are gone
The rain hasn't stopped since we were last together
Standing in the same room as you, trying to say goodbye
Never wanting to find the right words nor should I bother
Because no words can help me understand why
The lonely assassin that stole the moments from you and I, waits to take me away to retrieve the moments
I have until the same rain subsides
But only until my redemption fades to atonement
And on the night I die, the lonely assassin will come
My ever lasting loneliness will finally start to fade
I may not believe in a life after this one
But I still hope that I can retrieve one moment that stayed

Flight Of The Raven

i Look Up To The Sky

When you fly to close to the sun
When life and death become one
When life feels less than a haven
That's flight of the raven

Born to lose and live to win
And all you do is a sin
Nothing you do ever seems right
That's the raven's flight

Decaying from the inside
And you try to run and hide
When you reach the brink of insane
Flying above, is the raven again

When you've reach to point of death
And you have nothing else left
You look up to the sky
You'll see the raven fly by

ii Never Thought I'd see you again

Its flight of the raven, I never thought I'd see you again
Why won't you go away?
Why are you here to stay?
Is this the end of days?
Is this where I fray?
Get this life away from me
Can't you see the pain in my eyes?

I Am The Raven

I expect you don't know how you've affected my life, my mind and my soul
I suspect you don't really care how you have either
To you I was in the way, to be there for your amusement, there to be tortured
You have no interest in my tears, my hate or my torment
And why would you? They've never burdened you nor will they ever
Years have passed and I'm but a distant memory of a blackened soul you created
But you should know, I may not be in your eyesight but I'm always around. I'm not a burden but I am there.
Because that's my tears bleeding from your wounds, that's my hate that's fuelling your paranoia, that's my torment that leads to your death

Letting Go

i Holding On

Holding on is over rated
Holding on to long, becomes out dated
I surrender, I suffer
And I'll suffer forever

ii Because

I'm holding on to what makes me strong
I'm holding on, but you're already gone
For this I already know
Because the hardest part of holding on, is letting go

Wishing Life Away

We spend our days wishing life away
For the next big moment, to our next pay day
From new years resolution to birthday celebrations
An evening with friends, hoping it never ends
A life wished away, surely is a life wasted
Especially when moments come and we hesitated
Regrets removing time, which have little to spare
Reminding us that the moments we do have, we should care.

House Of Cards

The house of cards
Have fallen to shards
Of glass upon the floor

The shards remain
And begin to stain
Signifying that there is no more

The joker and the king
The redemption song they will sing
Laughing off gestures of war

The king and the joker
Gamble with the vulture
And now the house is no more

The Hanging Disappointment

Tied around my neck is your disappointment
Slightly choking me, but bearable
I don't like that you are, but I am what I am and I am unable to stop it
The stool beneath me is old and worn by your scorn that flows within your words
My poor choice of actions sways me back and forth
Causing scorn to flow, I can't stop the wearing of the stool nor can I stop my actions
The more I sway the tighter your disappointment gets. So tight I begin to blackout. You stand there watching but never stop me. Watching and lurking.
You stare at me while I suffer and sealed with a kiss, the stool breaks.

The Face Of Redemption

Your pain seeps through your eyes
Helping you wear it as a disguise

Never showing an ounce of your pain
Even though I see it in you time and again

I stare into your seeping eyes for a while
I get distracted by your breathtaking smile

I've known you for such a long time
And I know you'll never be mine

The face of redemption will always haunt me
Because you'll never know how much pain I can see

The face of redemption exists because I made it so
And now your image is burnt into my words just so you know

Screaming Through A Stitched Mouth

I've been screaming for longer than a day
All my thoughts all at one moment I want to say
Every society imbalance I want to portray
Religious impurities to stop them from their nightly pray

To expose the worlds insecurities for everyone to read
Let everyone watch while my wrists bleed
Stopping to inept and inadequate breed
Cutting off the ignorant from their media feed

My mouth maybe closed and stitched
But I can still read and see and feel enough to itch
And scratch, and leave me to die in a ditch
But next time you'll have to try harder to keep my mouth stitched

Dreaming Blind

A dream woke me up today with fear trickling down my spine, as sweat and the unknown
Not knowing where I am or what I'm doing, Who I am or what I'm seeing
Saving myself from conspiracy thoughts and the unjustified courts
The remedy, killing more than the disease
Wondering whose laws to appease, who's right or who's wrong
Finding sanctuary in the unknown and the unwanted, finding death as it lay dismembered in front of the sacred ground I bare
Upon my sight that fades in the light to the sightless lair

Anhedonic

What does it mean when you are unable to enjoy any aspect of your life?
Taking everything and everyone for granted and having the only expectation of them is that their only going to leave when you need them the most

An inability or want to share something as simple as the day or your birth or celebration with anyone with people who love and care for you, without thinking that there is an underlying reason for their want of you in their lives

Forever feeling disposable and at any minute you'll be thrown. When your biggest fear is to be own your own and left to your thoughts. That you have nothing to offer anyone and question why your there instead of enjoying that you are

Elmers End

Living in Elmers End
There doesn't seem to be a social trend
But I don't seem to be it

A lot of staring eyes
None of which I compromise
But I'm looked at like shit

Those compromising eyes stare at my friends
As well as I, but we live to meet no ends
Just to exist and die in peace

We live a rock'n'roll cliché
From excess drink, the music and girls we lay
In a small place with the faceless and the sleaze

Stabbed To Death (In The Sun)

It's hard to imagine the worst part of being a knife crime victim
Be it kicking screaming, drawing your last breath for your mum
Or forever being dubbed a statistic on the front page of The Sun

Neither crime seems to be related nor from one starting to provoke
But only one seeming trend in the victor can walk around and gloat
"I stabbed that guy in the chest last night, but I was aiming for the throat"

Who will be the next victim clutching their wound struggling for breath?
Will this be the linking story The Sun needs that they admit they're obsessed?
Nothing is for certain of who'll be the next person to be stabbed to death

Minerva's Reverie

Minerva's reverie
As pure as my words can be
Casting a shadow over the past
Hoping my words will ever last

Through all pages of history
Like Cummings, Poe and Duffy
Controlling how I hold my pen
Linking up the lives of all men

With every word I squander
Hoping all life will ponder
Over each and every inadequacy
That'll be Minerva's reverie

Good Morning My Someone

I've only just entered your mind and already I'm intrigued to see what else I can find
The smile your wear for comfort of self
Conversing misery that starts to engulf
Everything I ever know or understand
I've waited all my life to be your man
We only met one night in the middle of bedlam
But somehow you've awoken and became my someone

Sea Of Fire

Drowning in flames
Burning in the sea
Life isn't what you expected
Nor will it ever be

A hopeless romantic
To an audience who didn't want to know
But the romance continues
To finish off the show

Playing out this want
To end the words misery
To dowse the flames
And delay effigy

Breathing life into the lungs
Of all that almost drowned
Into the loveless, the unwanted
But still eternally profound

The embers are relighting
Smoke begins to rise
The tide is coming in
Announcing passions demise

We all try to stop
What will always be inevitable
To play out an encore
That won't help at all

Misery

I seem to spend my life making excuses for the way I act
But who am I to explain if my unhappiness is a fact

I've used everything I can claim to be a remedy
And I still come across chronically unhappy

Felling lethargic and down, prompts questions I don't need
Answering them all, is more effort than I can bleed

I can not be what you want me to be
I 'm not here to be fixed, so just leave me in my misery

The Angel Of Darkness

The curse of the dark angel
Is nothing less than a fable
He spends his life alone
Bringing kings to their throne

Living through the life he wants
But his words are an indescribable font
The angel wants to save
But to the darkness he is a slave

Surrounded by people alone alike
But no one carries on the fight
To stop rage growing in us all
And resist the rise and fall

The darkness is only here
Until he is understood with no fear
Before the angel of darkness is engulfed by the dead
Because what a sad life he would have lead

He's died before, maybe once or twice
With no control over his vice
Alone we all break
To prevent and forsake

Of Forever Dying

Of shadows that cover every will to be
Of remorse that is everything we want to see
Of decadence of what we want to be and never see
Of omens which destroy every passion that ever existed
Of Orion of the future and all the flowers that wilted

But tenderness it's everything we ever wanted in life and strife but never entered

Final Goodbye (For Now)

I sit here thinking of what to say
Trying to sum up our lives with you
And now our lives without you
Looking for the appropriate send off
But my mind draws a blank
Because nothing I write
And no poetic verse seems right

Too many days have passed and in no way
Can I comprehend you not here
Too many years and the comprehension still won't have sunk in
The only words I can say, feel
And believe is I love you and I'll see you soon
So this is my final goodbye (for now)

Until The End

My beautiful melody of redemption hasn't stopped
But more moved to a different song, a different tragedy to bestow on the world
I've sung these verses to death
Repeating myself over and over again
Like dancing echoes and shy shadows

The end is almost here
The infernal end we fear
But death isn't so lucky this time around
I won't be taken until everyone hears my sound
Deafening the world surrounding me
And everyone will finally see
I'm not dead and nor will I ever be

Michael Rosé

www.ingramcontent.com/pod-product-compliance
Lightning Source LLC
Chambersburg PA
CBHW051718040426
42446CB00008B/952